HIDDEN TREASURE QUEST

KNOWING GOD THROUGH JESUS

STUDY GUIDE

Hide and Seek Ministries

HSM

Hidden Treasure Quest: Knowing God Through Jesus Study Guide

ISBN: 978-0-9994901-6-7

Published by Hide and Seek Ministries
Springfield, MO 65801
www.hideandseekministries.com

TABLE OF CONTENTS

HIDDEN TREASURE QUEST

Proverbs 2:1-11

My son, accept my words.

Store up my commands inside you.

Let your ears listen to wisdom.

Apply your heart to understanding.

Call out for the ability to be wise.

Cry out for understanding.

Look for it as you would look for silver.

Search for it as you would search

for hidden treasure.

Then you will understand how to

have respect for the Lord.

You will find out how to know God.

The Lord gives wisdom.

Knowledge and understanding come from his mouth.

He stores up success for honest people.

He is like a shield to those who live without blame.

He guards the path of those who are honest.

He watches over the way of his faithful ones.

You will understand what is right and honest and fair.

You will understand the right way to live.

Your heart will become wise.

Your mind will delight in knowledge.

Good sense will keep you safe.

Understanding will guard you.

(NIrV, emphasis added)

INTRODUCTION

What is *Hidden Treasure Quest*?

Hidden Treasure Quest is a Christian discipleship series for ages nine to 14. The books are designed to guide readers in developing their **own** relationship with the Lord while learning how to apply God's Word to their lives and follow Jesus Christ.

What is the *Hidden Treasure Quest Study Guide*?

This Study Guide is an optional book intended to be used while reading *Hidden Treasure Quest: Knowing God Through Jesus*. The Study Guide provides questions and bible activities for each chapter of the book. The book and Study Guide are great resources to use at home, in church, in group study, or in the classroom.

How are the questions designed?

For each chapter, this guide includes three or more pages of questions and activities.

Review Questions: These questions will help readers review what they read in each chapter of the *Hidden Treasure Quest* book.

Bible Study Questions: These questions require additional study and readers usually need to use their Bible to find the answers. Some of these questions may require adult help depending on the age of the reader.

Chapter Activities: These activities are a fun way to reinforce the topics found in each chapter. Instructions are provided for most activities.

What materials will you need?

To complete the questions and activities in this guide, readers will need the book titled *Hidden Treasure Quest: Knowing God Through Jesus*, a version of the Bible that they can understand, a dictionary, a pen or pencil, crayons or colored pencils, a glue stick, scissors, and one piece of construction paper.

How can I use this Study Guide in a church setting or as homeschool curriculum?

The *Hidden Treasure Quest* books and Study Guides can be used as homeschool curriculum. Read and study at your own pace, or download the free *Teacher's Guide* for suggested lesson plans.

The books can also be used in a church setting. They work well for study on Sunday nights, Wednesday nights, in youth groups, or in small groups. They can also be utilized Sunday mornings depending on the church setting. The free *Teacher's Guide* assists leaders with suggested lesson plans, and the free *Church Guide* provides additional information about the series.

HSM offers church discounts. Prior to ordering, contact HSM to receive a coupon code for your church/church group.

Teachers have permission to photocopy pages in this Study Guide for the purpose of teaching others in a classroom setting.

To download a free *Church Guide* and/or *Teacher's Guide*, visit the HSM website: www.hideandseekministries.com/books.

Name:_____ **Date:**_____

A NOTE FROM BEN: REVIEW QUESTIONS

1. In Matthew 7:13-14, it says there are two roads that people choose to follow. What are the two roads?

    1. _____

    2. _____

2. Which road leads to Jesus?

_____

3. When you believe in Jesus, you are also choosing to _____ Him.

4. Can anyone force you to follow Jesus? Why or why not?

_____

_____

_____

5. What is your "map" to help you follow Jesus?

    a. Your school textbooks

    b. The Bible

    c. The internet

    d. All of the above

Name:_____ **Date:**_____

A NOTE FROM BEN: BIBLE STUDY QUESTIONS

In the books of Matthew, Mark, Luke and John, the Bible talks about following Jesus at least 76 times. **Read** about six of those times by looking up the following verses in your Bible.

☐ Matthew 4:19-20   ☐ John 8:12

☐ Matthew 9:9   ☐ John 10:27

☐ Matthew 16:24   ☐ John 12:26

The Bible also says this in 1 Peter 2:21:

> "To this you were called, because Christ suffered for you, leaving you an example, <u>that you should follow in his steps</u>."
> (NIV underline added)

One of the Greek words in the Bible for "follow" (as in following Jesus) is *akoloutheo* (ak-ol-oo-theh-oh). Its meaning gives the idea of "being on the same roadway with someone".[1] Following Jesus on His "road" is the only way to Heaven. Although there is not a literal road, how does a person get on the "road" to Heaven? (Hint: Read John 14:6, Romans 10:9, and Ephesians 2:8.)

_____

_____

_____

_____

_____

_____

[1] Jack W. Hayford et al., eds., *New Spirit Filled Life Bible*. (Nashville: Thomas Nelson Publishers, 2002), 1469.

We will read a lot about what it means to follow Jesus in this book. And it's important to know what our "map" says as we follow Him. Psalm 119:105 says:

"Your word is a lamp to my feet And a light to my path." (NKJV)

Why do you think it's important to use God's Word as your "map" to follow Jesus?

_____

_____

_____

_____

_____

This book is titled *Knowing God Through Jesus*. Why does learning about Jesus also help us learn about God? (If you need help, read John 8:19 and 14:5-11).

_____

_____

_____

_____

_____

_____

JOE IS LOST.
HELP HIM FIND THE RIGHT ROAD TO FOLLOW.

Start

Finish

"Your word is a lamp to my feet
And a light to my path."
(Psalm 119:105 NKJV)

Name:_____ **Date:**_____

CHAPTER 1: REVIEW QUESTIONS

1. Eve started paying more attention to _____ than she did the voice of God.

    a. her favorite book

    b. Adam

    c. the serpent's voice

2. What are some "voices" that can speak to people? (Circle all that apply.)

    a. Television

    b. Books

    c. Radio

    d. The internet

    e. Other people

3. God is speaking to you right now.

    a. True

    b. False

4. Who is the Shepherd? _____

5. Who are the sheep? _____

6. As with Eve, what you pay attention to affects the _____ you make.

Name:_____ Date:_____

CHAPTER 1: BIBLE STUDY QUESTIONS

Sheep need a lot of water to survive. If a shepherd does not lead them to a clean water source, the sheep will find other places to drink water such as a mud puddle. And drinking dirty water can be harmful to the sheep. Sheep need a shepherd to show them where to find clean water.

Read what Jesus said about being thirsty and drinking water.

- "If anyone thirsts, let him come to Me and drink." (John 7:37 NKJV)

- "He who believes in Me shall never thirst." (John 6:35 NKJV)

- "Blessed are those who hunger and thirst for righteousness, For they shall be filled [satisfied]." (Matthew 5:6 NKJV)

- "Whoever drinks of this water will thirst again, but whoever drinks of the water that I shall give him will never thirst. But the water that I shall give him will become in him a fountain of water springing up into everlasting life." (John 4:13-14 NKJV).

Read that last verse again in John 4. Why do you think we will never thirst again if we drink the water that Jesus has? Is Jesus talking about actual water that we put in a cup? The answer is *no*. When Jesus talks about being thirsty, He is talking about the things we want or desire.

On the following lines, write some things that you want in this world. (Maybe it's books, toys, movies, games, a bicycle, jewelry or other things.)

_____

_____

_____

Jesus is not saying that wanting things in this world is bad. The problem comes when we think we can only be satisfied with the things that we want in this world. For example, a person might say, "If I get this one thing I will be so happy and never want another thing again." But that is never true. Jesus says we can never truly be satisfied or completely happy with things that are in this world. We will always keep wanting more and more. Another way to say it is we will keep being thirsty.

According to Jesus, what do we need to do to never be "thirsty" again?

_____

_____

_____

_____

Jesus says that His "water" offers "everlasting life". What does that mean?

_____

_____

_____

_____

We need Jesus as our Shepherd to lead us to the water that Jesus has, so we are not drinking out of mud puddles like real sheep do. To make Jesus our Shepherd, we need to listen to His voice instead of all the other "voices" in this world. This requires reading your Bible. Below, list a time of day (in your own life) that you can sit down in a quiet place and read your Bible every day. (For example: *I can get up early before school and read. I can read before I go to bed. I can read after dinner, alone in my room.*)

_____

WHAT'S IN YOUR FUTURE?

Pretend you have a time machine and you travel 20 years in the future. Draw a picture of what you think you might be doing 20 years from now.

My age in 20 years: _____

Year
_____

Do you think that God's plans or your plans are better for your future?_____

FOR I KNOW THE PLANS I HAVE FOR YOU," DECLARES THE LORD, "PLANS TO PROSPER YOU AND NOT TO HARM YOU, PLANS TO GIVE YOU HOPE AND A FUTURE. (JEREMIAH 29:11 NIV)

Name:_____ **Date:**_____

CHAPTER 2: REVIEW QUESTIONS

1. When Jesus looks at people, He looks at _____.

    a. the way they look

    b. how many things they have

    c. their heart

2. Proverbs 4:23 says everything you do comes from _____.

    a. your mind

    b. your heart

    c. your spirit

3. What can your heart do? (Circle all that apply.)

    a. think   d. believe   g. have fear

    b. doubt   e. make decisions   h. have joy

    c. love   f. have faith   i. have courage

4. According to Proverbs 27:19, your life is like a _____ to your heart.

    a. key

    b. book

    c. computer

    d. mirror

Name: _____ **Date:** _____

CHAPTER 2: BIBLE STUDY QUESTIONS

Read John 8:1-11.

Did Jesus see the woman differently than the men did? _____

When the men looked at the woman, all they could see was the bad thing she had done. But what do you think Jesus saw when He looked at the woman?

_____

_____

_____

This doesn't mean that Jesus just ignored the bad thing the woman did. Jesus does not like sin. However, read what the Bible says in 1 John.

"But God is faithful and fair. If we confess our sins, he will forgive our sins. He will forgive every wrong thing we have done. He will make us pure." (1 John 1:9 NIrV)

Do you think Jesus could see that the woman was sorry for what she had

done? _____

If someone does something wrong to you, should you stay upset with them and always remember the bad thing they did to you every time you see them? Or, should you look at them differently: forgive the way Jesus forgives them, and see them the way Jesus sees them?

_____

_____

_____

Read Acts 3:1-10. There was a man who had not been able to walk for his entire life, and he was brought to the temple every day so he could beg for money. Many people in the city had seen him there numerous times and recognized who he was. It was likely that Peter and John had also seen the man at the temple many times before. So, what was different about this particular day that we read about in Acts 3? Why did Peter and John talk to the man on that day and not other days?

Not long before this, Jesus was raised from the dead. And in Acts 2, it says after Jesus went back to Heaven, Peter, John and the other disciples received the Holy Spirit. In other words, Peter and John now had Jesus living inside them. Jesus helped Peter and John see the man near the temple differently than they had before. If you believe in Jesus, He also lives inside you and will help you see people the way He sees them.

Read John 14:26 and write the verse below.

_____

_____

_____

_____

DRAW THE MIRROR IMAGES
OF THESE CREATURES

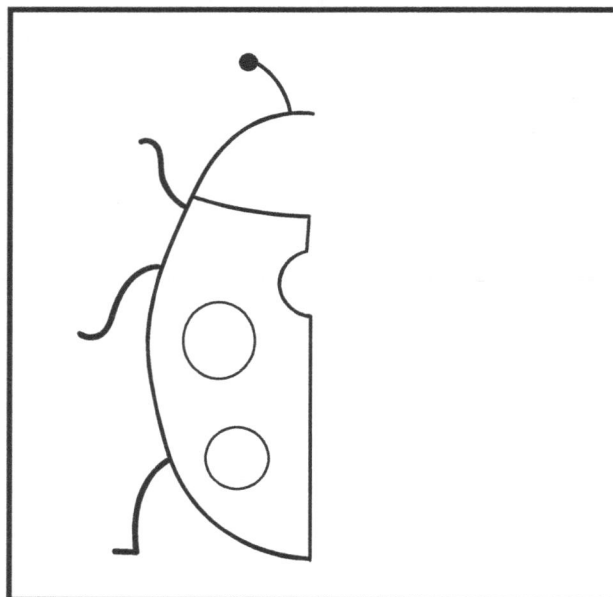

**As water reflects the face, so one's life reflects the heart.
Proverbs 27:19 NIV**

Name:_____ **Date:**_____

CHAPTER 3: REVIEW QUESTIONS

1. John 3:16 says, "For God so loved the world that he gave his one and

only _____ (NIV)."

2. When Jesus came to earth, He was fully God but He was also fully human.

    a. True

    b. False

3. The Bible says Jesus bought you at a price (1 Cor. 6:20). Jesus didn't use

money to buy you. What did He use? _____

4. The Bible says, "This is how we know what _____ is: Jesus Christ
laid down his life for us" (1 John 3:16 NIV).

    a. God's Word

    b. love

    c. the Holy Spirit

5. When Jesus was getting ready to die, He went through so many horrible
things that He didn't look like a man anymore.

    a. True

    b. False

Name:_____ **Date:**_____

CHAPTER 3: BIBLE STUDY QUESTIONS

The Bible says, "God is love" (1 John 4:8). Read the following verses from 1 Corinthians 13 aloud. Every time it says "love" say the word "God" instead.

Love is patient, *love* is kind. [*Love*] does not envy, [*love*] does not boast, [*love*] is not proud. [*Love*] is not rude, [*love*] is not self-seeking, [*love*] is not easily angered, [*love*] keeps no account of wrongs. *Love* takes no pleasure in evil, but rejoices in the truth. [*Love*] bears all things, believes all things, hopes all things, endures all things. *Love* never fails. (1 Cor. 13:4-8 NIV brackets added)

Jesus said, "You must love one another, just as I have loved you." (John 13:34 NIrV). What are some things you can do to love the way Jesus loves? (Hint: Look at the verses in 1 Corinthians 13 above.)

_____

_____

_____

_____

_____

_____

_____

_____

In 1 John 3:18 it says:

"Let us not love with words or speech but with actions and in truth." (NIV)

Another version says:

"Don't just talk about love. Put your love into action. Then it will truly be love." (NIrV)

In your own words, what do you think this verse means?

_____

_____

_____

_____

Jesus put His love into action many times while He was on earth. **Read the following verses.**

☐ John 15:13   ☐ Romans 5:8   ☐ Ephesians 5:2

What is Jesus' greatest act of love?

_____

_____

_____

_____

FIND THE HIDDEN TREASURE

A two-player game. Each player decides where to hide their treasure on the map below. Write down the location on a piece of paper. Do not show the other player. Each player takes turns trying to find the other player's treasure by calling out grid squares (such as F5). Track where you've guessed with a crayon. The first player to find the treasure wins.

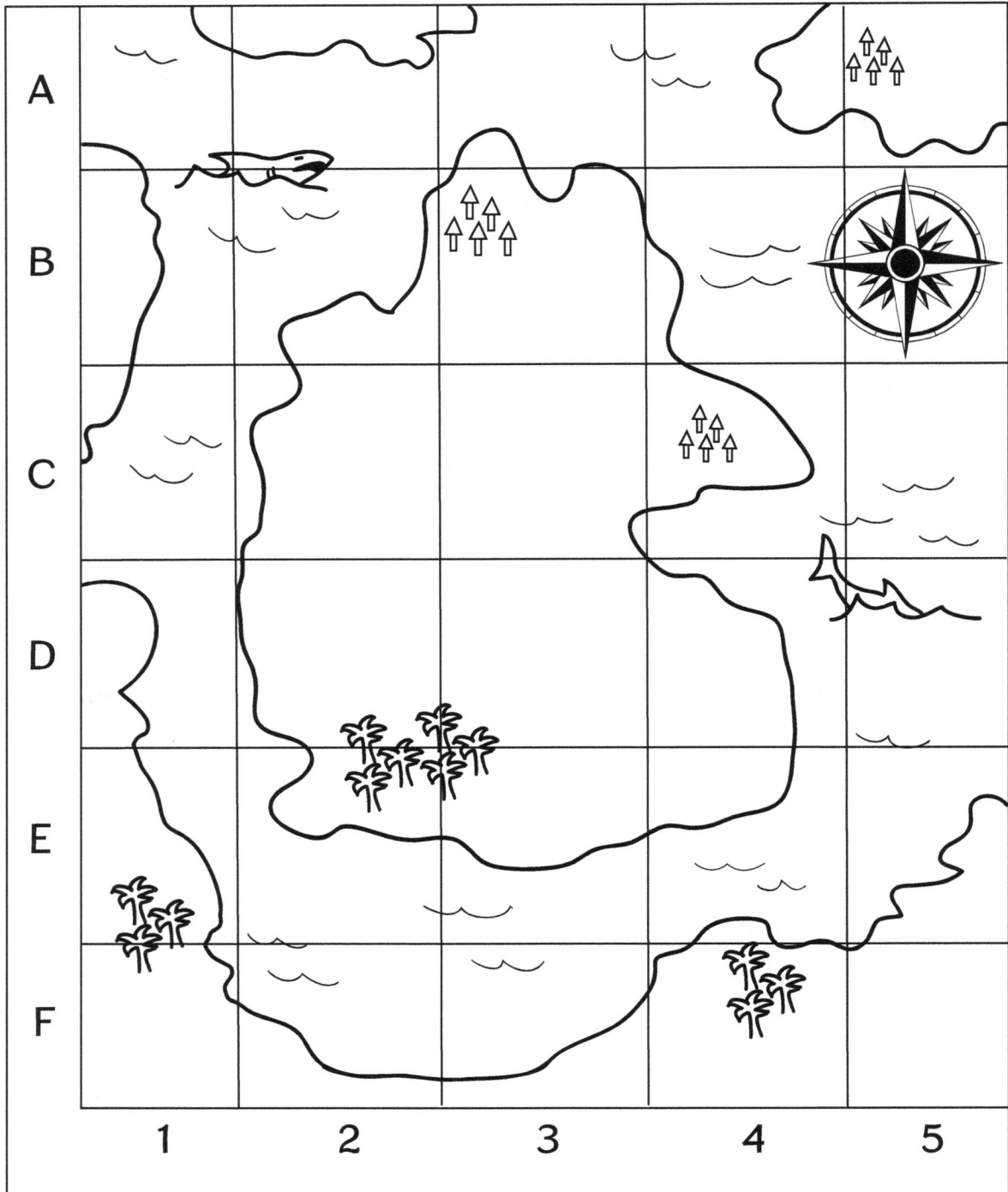

MATTHEW 13:44

Name:_____ Date:_____

CHAPTER 4: REVIEW QUESTIONS

1. The Bible says, "Don't live the way the world lives" (Rom. 12:2 NIrV). Who is the "world"?

    a. Every person who is alive

    b. Those who believe in Jesus

    c. Those who do not believe in Jesus

2. If you are following the will of God, you will notice a difference between the way you act and the way the world acts.

    a. True

    b. False

3. The Bible says those who do not believe in Jesus are in _____.

    a. the clouds

    b. the light

    c. darkness

4. Jesus said, "I am the _____ of the world" (John 8:12 NKJV).

    a. man

    b. wisdom

    c. light

5. Jesus said all people who believe in Him are the _____ of the world.

    a. light

    b. darkness

Name:_____ **Date:**_____

CHAPTER 4: BIBLE STUDY QUESTIONS

Read Acts 8:26-40. The Ethiopian man worked for a queen who believed in God. And the Bible tells us he was in Jerusalem where people went to the temple to worship God. The Ethiopian likely heard about Jesus while He was there. After being in Jerusalem, the Ethiopian was now interested in what the Bible says, and Philip found him reading it. However, even though he was reading it, he was having a hard time understanding it.

When Philip first saw the man, was the Ethiopian living in the light or in darkness? How do you know?

_____

_____

How did Philip act as a light for the Ethiopian? (Hint: Read Acts 8:35.)

_____

_____

_____

Philip did not force the Ethiopian to believe in Jesus. He simply "opened his mouth" and spoke to him about Jesus (Acts 8:35 NKJV). Because Philip did this, the Ethiopian went from living in darkness to living in the light. This was possible because Phillip opened his mouth and spoke the Word of God. **Read Psalm 119:105** and copy the verse below.

_____

_____

_____

What do you think it means that the Bible lights our path and helps us see where to go?

_____

_____

_____

_____

_____

In Acts 8, Phillip used God's Word to light the path of the Ethiopian and helped the man see where to go. Opening your mouth and speaking God's Word (or speaking about God's Word) is one way to be a light in this world. Can you think of other ways you can be a light?

_____

_____

_____

_____

_____

_____

_____

_____

_____

WORD SEARCH

```
S  B  S  Z  X  C  K  W  K  H  X  A  B  J
S  Q  L  E  H  D  N  L  E  P  S  O  G  L
E  L  G  I  C  P  A  T  H  G  M  S  I  E
N  M  C  P  N  I  A  D  Y  R  A  G  K  N
K  W  E  D  Q  D  O  K  W  D  H  K  U  T
R  O  N  L  H  P  E  H  F  T  B  X  Z  T
A  R  O  G  N  S  H  D  C  I  F  E  J  R
D  L  O  E  M  H  B  E  T  O  U  T  E  N
S  D  N  H  V  N  R  A  A  L  R  L  P  Q
D  I  F  F  E  R  E  N  T  R  B  I  P  F
Q  P  S  F  E  O  E  V  X  I  T  T  W  Q
N  X  N  M  Q  U  Q  J  B  V  C  H  W  A
```

BIBLE	GOSPEL
BLINDED	HEART
CHOICES	LIGHT
DARKNESS	PATH
DIFFERENT	WORLD

"I am the light of the world. He who follows Me shall not walk in darkness, but have the light of life."
(John 8:12 NKJV)

Name:_____ **Date:**_____

CHAPTER 5: REVIEW QUESTIONS

1. Another way to say that you are doing God's will is you are following God's path.

    a. True

    b. False

2. The _____ determine whether you follow God's path.

    a. foods you cook

    b. choices you make

    c. people you live with

    d. type of Bible you read

3. If you believe in Jesus you will always follow God's path. (Hint: There is only One who has followed God's path perfectly.)

    a. True

    b. False

4. List some things you can do to seek God. (Read pages 28-29 in Chapter 5.)

_____

_____

_____

_____

_____

Name:_____ **Date:**_____

CHAPTER 5: BIBLE STUDY QUESTIONS

Proverbs 14:12 says, "There is a way that seems right to a man, But its end is the way of death" (NKJV). In other words, just because something may seem like the "right" thing to do, does not mean that it is. How can we know if something is the right thing to do?

_____

_____

_____

_____

You likely thought of good answers to the question above. But the best way to know if something is the right thing to do is to ask the question, *"Does it match what the Bible says?"* Another way to say it is this: imagine if you could see Jesus sitting right next to you in your living room. Would you be completely comfortable with telling Him about all the things you do, the words you say, the things you think about, and the things you listen to? Would you talk to Him about all the places you go, let Him hear all the words you say, and tell Him about all the thoughts you think?

No one (except for Jesus) is able to follow God's path perfectly. Even after we decide to believe in Jesus, we still make mistakes. What do you think you should do if you realize you've made a bad choice that Jesus would not approve of?

_____

_____

_____

_____

_____

_____

_____

In Romans 5:8 it says, "But here is how God has shown his love for us. While we were still sinners, Christ died for us" (NIrV). When God sent Jesus to die for you, He already knew about every bad thing you would ever do. God loves you no matter what you do, what you say, or what you think. However, bad things (or bad choices) can get in the way of your relationship with God. They can keep you from staying on the path that God has for you, and you can miss out on many wonderful things. What is something you can do right now that will help you seek God and know Him better?

_____

_____

_____

_____

Read Jeremiah 29:13 and write the verse below.

_____

_____

_____

_____

SOLVE THE CODE

A	B	C	D	E	F	G	H	I	J	K	L	M
26	25	24	23	22	21	20	19	18	17	16	15	14

N	O	P	Q	R	S	T	U	V	W	X	Y	Z
13	12	11	10	9	8	7	6	5	4	3	2	1

In ___ ___ ___ your ways
   26 15 15

___ ___ ___ ___ ___ ___ ___ ___ ___ ___ ___ Him,
26 24 16 13 12 4 15 22 23 20 22

and He shall ___ ___ ___ ___ ___ ___
            23 18 9 22 24 7

your ___ ___ ___ ___ ___.   PROVERS 3:6
    11 26 7 19 8   (NKJV)

Look up the word "acknowledge" in the dictionary and write its meaning below.

_____

_____

_____

_____

Name:_____   **Date:**_____

CHAPTER 6: REVIEW QUESTIONS

1. The disciples saw Jesus feed 5,000 people with very little food. Later, Jesus wanted to feed 4,000 people. Why did the disciples not understand how Jesus could feed 4,000 people when they had already seen Him feed 5,000?

_____

_____

_____

_____

2. List some things in life that can distract you.

_____

_____

_____

_____

3. Distractions can make you lose your focus on God and leave God's path.

    a. True

    b. False

4. What is one thing you can do to help you keep your focus on God?

_____

_____

_____

Name:_____ Date:_____

CHAPTER 6: BIBLE STUDY QUESTIONS

Read the following verses about remembering what God has done.

- ☐ Deuteronomy 6:12
- ☐ Deuteronomy 8:18
- ☐ Psalm 105:5

Read the following verses about remembering what Jesus has said and done.

- ☐ John 16:4
- ☐ Luke 22:17-20
- ☐ 2 Timothy 2:8

God has always wanted His people to remember what He has done. Remembering helps you keep your focus on God and helps you stay on the right path.

Think of the two times Jesus fed thousands of people with a small amount of food. The disciples did not believe (or have faith) that Jesus could feed the 4,000 even though they had seen Him feed 5,000. They didn't believe because they didn't remember what Jesus had already done. With this is mind, how does remembering what God has done help build up your faith?

_____

_____

_____

_____

_____

_____

_____

_____

The Bible tells you to remember. But the Bible also says that God remembers. Psalm 105:8 says, "[God] remembers his covenant forever, the promise he made, for a thousand generations" (NIV). God never forgets what He has promised you, and He never breaks His promises. It is impossible for God to lie (Heb. 6:18). This is an amazing truth!

However, there is something that God does <u>not</u> remember. **Read** the following verses in your Bible.

    ☐ Isaiah 43:25
    ☐ Acts 3:19

Write what God does <u>not</u> remember on the lines below.

_____

_____

_____

_____

If someone does _not_ believe in Jesus, does God remember their sins?

_____

_____

_____

Think about things you have read in the Bible. And think about things that have happened in your own life. On the lines below, list some things God has done that will help you build up your faith when you remember them.

_____

_____

_____

_____

_____

_____

_____

_____

_____

_____

_____

6. **Read John 14:26.** Who will help you remember things?

_____

_____

MEMORY GAME

Color the pictures below. Cut along the single dotted line to remove this page from this book. Glue the page onto construction paper (so the page is no longer see-through). Cut out each square, and then play a memory game! Place all pieces face down on a table. Each player takes turns flipping two squares over. If the player finds a match, they can keep the cards. If no match is found, turn the cards face down again. The player with the most matches at the end of the game wins.

Name:_____ **Date:**_____

CHAPTER 7: REVIEW QUESTIONS

1. List seven reasons why we should pray.

1. _____

2. _____

3. _____

4. _____

5. _____

6. _____

7. _____

2. Describe one example from the Bible that shows how prayer changes things.

_____

_____

_____

_____

3. The example prayer that Jesus prayed in Matthew 6 is called _____.

   a. The Only Prayer of Jesus

   b. The Lord's Prayer

   c. The Disciples' Prayer

Name:_____ **Date:**_____

CHAPTER 7: BIBLE STUDY QUESTIONS

In Chapter 7, you read how prayer and the Bible work together. For the next four days, let's see how this works in your own life. Starting today, take your Bible to a quiet place with no distractions. Then, before you open your Bible, start talking with God. You can pray about anything you want to. Remember, your prayers delight Him (Prov. 15:8). He loves to hear from you. Thank Him for things, tell Him what you need, and ask for help to hear Him as you read His Word. When you're done praying, read a chapter (or more) in your Bible.

When you're done reading, sit in the quiet and listen for a while. Sometimes when you're reading the Bible, the Holy Spirit can give you what some would call a "quickening" in your spirit. In other words, you read something in the Bible and you are very sure that the verses you just read are specifically for you at that moment. It is also possible to hear God speak words to you or show you things in your spirit.

However, don't get discouraged if you do not hear anything. Remember, when we pray we should not only pray just because we want something from God. We should pray because we love God, and we talk with the ones we love. Pray because you want to spend time with God. Most importantly, don't give up. Keep reading and praying every day.

Here is a list of chapters for you to read during the next four days.

- ☐ Day one: Matthew 25
- ☐ Day two: Matthew 26
- ☐ Day three: Matthew 27
- ☐ Day four: Matthew 28

You should continue to pray and read the Bible even after the next four days are over. And you could even do this multiple times per day. In doing this, you will be making an effort to seek God and stay on His path.

In Chapter 7, you also read that thanking God is a way to battle Satan. If you spend time thanking God, it means that you are remembering what He has done for you (like we read in Chapter 6). We know that remembering what God has done helps build up our faith. Why is building up your faith a way to fight against (or resist) Satan?

_____

_____

_____

_____

_____

In Chapter 7, you also read that Jesus prayed for other people. On the lines below, make a list of people that you want to remember to pray for.

_____

_____

_____

_____

_____

COLOR BY NUMBER

1 - brown
2 - red
3 - orange
4 - purple
5 - blue
6 - green
7 - yellow

BUT THE PRAYER OF THE
UPRIGHT IS HIS DELIGHT.
PROVERBS 15:8 (NKJV)

Name:_____ **Date:**_____

CHAPTER 8: REVIEW QUESTIONS

1. Where does God hide His wisdom and knowledge?

    a. He buried them in the ground.

    b. He hid them in Jesus.

    c. It's a secret. No one knows.

2. If you believe in Jesus, God's wisdom and knowledge are inside you.

    a. True

    b. False

3. What part of your body is like a faucet?

    a. Your feet

    b. Your eyes

    c. Your mind

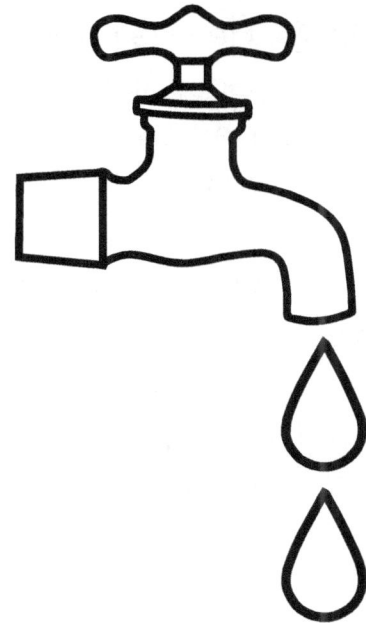

4. What is the "water" inside you?

    a. God's wisdom and knowledge

    b. Your thoughts and dreams

    c. Your words

5. How do you turn on your "faucet"?

_____

_____

_____

_____

Name:_____ **Date:**_____

CHAPTER 8: BIBLE STUDY QUESTIONS

Read Acts 8:9-25. Simon used to be a sorcerer. (A person who claimed to have magic powers that were evil.) As a sorcerer, Simon had gained a lot of knowledge from the "world". He knew how to use evil power to "astonish" people (Acts 8:9 NKJV). He was so good at what he did and had so much worldy knowledge, that people thought he had "the great power of God" (Acts 8:10 NKJV). But then Philip came to his town, and the people saw what the true power of God was like.

The Bible says Simon later decided to believe in Jesus and he was baptized (Acts 8:13). He was no longer a sorcerer. However, instead of learning about the ways of God, Simon continued to think and act using the knowledge that he had received from the world. Simon was focused on worldly things and not on godly things.

No matter how old a person is, they will continue to have opportunities to learn new things. And even if you believe in Jesus, you will always have a choice between learning the right way and the wrong way. Just as Adam and Eve received the knowledge of good *and* evil, you also have that opportunity. Are you going to choose to learn the ways of the world or the ways of God?

In your own life, answer the following questions honestly and the best you can. Pick a day of the week. During that day, how much time do you spend:

watching television or movies?_____

playing with some type of toy or game?_____

doing sports or physical activities?_____

doing school work? _____

spending time with family or friends? _____

During that same day, how much time do you spend praying and reading the Bible?_____

Every time you interact with the world (such as watching television, reading books, or playing with friends at school), you are taking in the world's knowledge. However, you live in this world, and there is no way to get away from all worldly knowledge. Plus, not everything (or everyone) in this world is bad. The important question is: how much time are you spending with God compared to how much time you are spending with the world? Is God most important in your life? If you are spending twelve hours per day taking in the world's knowledge and only five minutes per day taking in God's knowledge, whose knowledge do you think you will end up following?

We read in Acts 8 that Simon continued to think and act with his worldly knowledge even after he believed in Jesus. **Read the following verses.**

☐ Romans 12:2   ☐ James 1:5   ☐ Proverbs 2:1-11

☐ Joshua 1:8   ☐ Psalm 1:1-2   ☐ Proverbs 4:20-27

What are some things you can do to "turn on your faucet" and think and act with your godly knowledge?

_____

_____

_____

_____

_____

_____

WORD SCRAMBLE

Unscramble each words in the boxes below.

RAED

☐☐☐☐
　　3

HTE

☐☐☐
12 13

IBBEL

☐☐☐☐☐

BOYE

☐☐☐☐
7

ETH

☐☐☐
2

ILBEB

☐☐☐☐☐

UGRAD

☐☐☐☐☐
6

ROUY

☐☐☐☐
4

EHATR

☐☐☐☐☐

SAK

☐☐☐
　1

OFR

☐☐☐

IWSODM

☐☐☐☐☐☐
　　　9　　5

RPYA

☐☐☐☐
10

VEEYR

☐☐☐☐☐

ADY

☐☐☐
8 11

Look at the words above. Find the letters with numbers below them.
In the boxes below, find the matching number and write the letter in that box.

☐☐☐☐ ☐N ☐☐☐☐ ☐☐☐☐
1 2 3 4 5 6 7 8 9 10 11 12 13

Name:_____ **Date:**_____

CHAPTER 9: REVIEW QUESTIONS

1. The Bible says while Jesus was on earth, He spent much of His time preaching, teaching, and _____.

    a. sleeping

    b. studying

    c. healing

2. The Bible tells us about all things that Jesus did while He was on earth.

    a. True

    b. False

3. While Jesus was on earth, He said He can only do what He sees God do. (In other words, if you want to know what God is like, read about the life of Jesus.)

    a. True

    b. False

4. As a follower of Jesus, it is possible for you to teach, preach, and heal just as Jesus did while He was on earth.

    a. True

    b. False

Name:_____ **Date:**_____

CHAPTER 9: BIBLE STUDY QUESTIONS

Read Acts 3:1-10. How did Peter do the same works as Jesus?

_____

_____

_____

_____

Read Acts 3:16. *How* did Peter say that he *was able* to do the same works as Jesus?

_____

_____

_____

Read Acts 2:43. Is healing the lame man the only time that Peter did the same works as Jesus?

_____

Read John 14:12, Acts 1:8, and Romans 8:11. Do you think it is possible that you can also do the same works as Jesus (and Peter)?

_____

The Bible says, "God's whole nature is living in Christ in human form" (Col. 2:9 NIrV). Jesus also said, "Very truly I tell you, the Son can do nothing by himself; he can do only what he sees his Father doing, because whatever the Father does the Son also does" (John 5:19 NIV). In other words, we can read about Jesus and learn about God.

Read John 8:1-12. As we read about Jesus in these verses, what can we learn about God?

_____

_____

_____

_____

_____

_____

Read John 9:1-7. As we read about Jesus in these verses, what can we learn about God?

_____

_____

_____

_____

_____

HIDDEN MESSAGE
WORD SEARCH

```
D  O  P  R  E  A  C  H  I  N  G
T  T  E  A  C  H  I  N  G  R  F
G  N  I  L  A  E  H  H  E  F  A
E  V  E  I  L  E  B  W  N  A  T
E  W  O  R  K  S  O  O  O  I  H
F  J  E  S  U  P  S  S  C  T  E
T  I  R  I  P  S  Y  L  O  H  R
```

✝
believe	Holy Spirit	Son
Father	power	teaching
healing	preaching	faith
✝

After finding all the words, write the letters you did not circle in order on the lines below to reveal the hidden message.

__ __   __ __   __ __ __ __ __   __ __   __ __ __ __ __

Name:_____ **Date:**_____

CHAPTER 10: REVIEW QUESTIONS

1. If you believe in Jesus, you are part of the body of _____.

2. There is one body but many different _____.

    a. parts

    b. feet

    c. spirits

3. All parts of the body of Christ are important.

    a. True

    b. False

4. God has given each person who believes in Him at least one gift. What is an example of those gifts?

    a. giving

    b. teaching

    c. encouraging others

    d. all of the above

5. List three places in the Bible where you can read about gifts from God?

_____

_____

_____

Name:_____ **Date:**_____

CHAPTER 10: BIBLE STUDY QUESTIONS

Read 1 Corinthians 12:12-26. You are a part in the body of Christ. Is your part more important than someone else's part?_____

The Pastor of your church is a part of the body of Christ. Is your Pastor's part more important than your part?_____

Missionaries who travel around the world are part of the body of Christ. Are their parts more important than your part? _____

There are people with the gift of miracles who are able to do amazing things through the power of the Holy Spirit. Is their part more important than yours?

_____

Read 1 Corinthians 12:4-6. Why is one person's part in the body of Christ <u>not</u> more important than another person's part?

> *There are different gifts and parts of the body, but they all come from the same _____.*

If you are a kid, is it bad that you do not know what your spiritual gifts are yet? (Hint: The answer is, "*No, it's not a bad thing. I still have time to learn what they are as I get older.*")

_____

_____

_____

In 1 Corinthians 12:25, it says, "so that there should be no division in the body, but that its parts should have equal concern for each other" (NIV). What does the word "division" mean? (Use a dictionary if you need help.)

_____

_____

_____

Although there are many parts of the body of Christ, the people in the body should not be divided. In other words, you should love <u>all</u> the other people who are in the body of Christ. Ephesians 5:29-30 says:

> "No one ever hates his own body, but feeds and takes care of it.
> And that is what Christ does for the church, because we are parts
> of his body" (NCV).

"No one ever hates his own body." If we are hungry, we eat. If we are thirsty, we drink. If we are cold, we do things to make ourselves warmer. We take care of our own bodies. In the same way, we are part of Jesus' body, and He will take care of us.

Furthermore, we should love other people in the body of Christ just as we would love and take care of our own bodies. Not only are everyone's gifts equally important, but other people's gifts are meant to help *you*. And your gifts are meant to help others.

In 1 Corinthians 12:7, it says, "The Holy Spirit is given to each of us in a special way. <u>That is for the good of all</u>" (NIrV underline added).

God gives us gifts so we can help each other. And as we use our gifts and follow the head of the body, we can work together in following God's path and not be divided.

SPIRITUAL GIFTS CROSSWORD

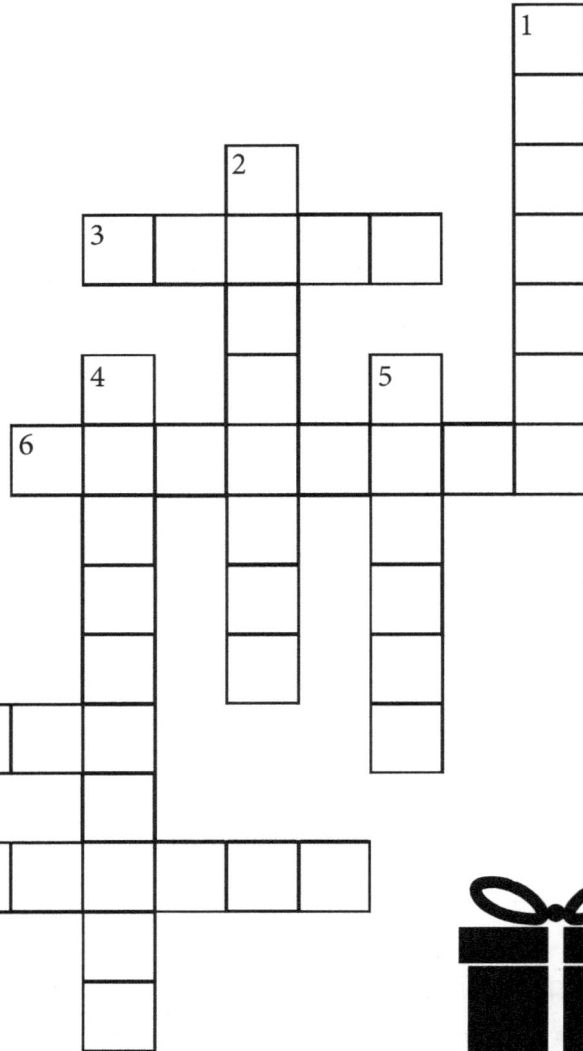

Word Bank

faith
giving
healing
leadership
miracles
pastor
prophecy
teaching

Across

3. Special gift of believing God without doubt
6. Special gift of explaining and applying truths from God
7. Special gift of caring for and preaching to the body of Christ
8. Special gift of speaking messages from God, especially about the future

Down

1. Special gift of helping a person become well
2. Special gift of displaying power, doing the impossible
4. Special gift of leading and developing those in the body of Christ
5. Special gift to give out of generosity

Note: This puzzle does not include all of the spiritual gifts that are found in the Bible.

Name:_____ **Date:**_____

CHAPTER 11: REVIEW QUESTIONS

1. Jesus' life is an example of what it is like to have faith.

    a. True. Jesus lived by faith.

    b. False. Jesus didn't need faith because He is God.

2. Do you need faith to see that your mother is sitting next to you? _____

3. Do you need faith to know that God is with you? _____

4. Faith works by being sure about something that you do not yet see.

    a. True

    b. False

5. Human faith works with your five _____.

6. The faith that comes from God works with your five senses.

    a. True

    b. False

7. You cannot use your human faith to believe godly things.

    a. True

    b. False

Name:_____ **Date:**_____

CHAPTER 11: BIBLE STUDY QUESTIONS

Read 1 Samuel 17:1-51. What did the men in the army do when they saw Goliath? (Hint: Read 1 Samuel 17:24 again.)

_____

Goliath was more than nine feet tall. His armor weighed about 125 pounds, and the end of his spear weighed about 15 pounds. He was mean, huge, very strong, and wasn't afraid to kill someone.

Read 1 Samuel 17:11 again. Were the Israelites using human faith or godly faith when deciding whether to fight Goliath? How do you know?

_____

_____

_____

_____

Read 1 Samuel 17:33-37 again. What kind of faith was King Saul using?

_____

What kind of faith was David using? _____

David had faith (or was absolutely sure) that he could defeat Goliath even though it seemed impossible. In 1 Samuel 17:33-37, what did David do to help build up his faith? (Hint: We read about it in Chapter 6.)

_____

_____

_____

_____

_____

When David decided not to wear any armor, what kind of faith was he using?

_____

Read what David said in 1 Samuel 17:45-47 again. The Bible says everything you do comes from your heart (Proverbs 4:23). Since this is true, the words David spoke came right from his heart. And in Chapter 3, we read that God chose David because of what was in his heart.

James 2:17 says, "Faith by itself, if it is not accompanied by action, is dead" (NIV). David had faith that God was stronger than Goliath, and God would help him defeat Goliath. But David did not just have faith in his heart. He also put his faith into action as it says in James 2:17.

For example, if you believe in Jesus but you've never told anyone else about Him, are you putting your faith into action?_____

Here's another example. Malachi 3:10 says that we should give ten percent of the money we receive back to God (called tithing). He says if we do this, He will pour out such a blessing that we won't have room for it all. If a person believes the whole Bible is true, but they have never tithed, are they putting their faith into action? _____

Remember, you should not just keep faith in your heart, but you should also put your faith into action just as David did when he fought Goliath.

FAITH

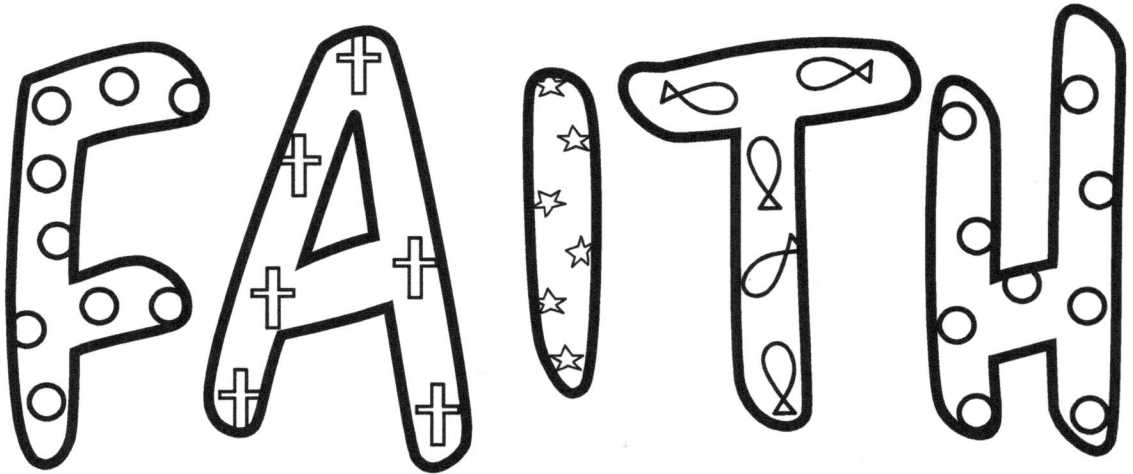

How many words can you make out of the letters in:

FAITH LIKE JESUS

_____   _____

_____   _____

_____   _____

_____   _____

_____   _____

_____   _____

_____   _____

_____   _____

Name:_____ Date:_____

CHAPTER 12: REVIEW QUESTIONS

1. The Bible is full of a long list of rules that are meant to make your life harder.

    a. True

    b. False

2. In Proverbs 8:31, it says Jesus _____ in you.

3. What does it mean to *delight* in another person?

_____

_____

_____

_____

4. To get to Heaven, you must obey the Bible perfectly.

    a. True

    b. False

5. Why should you do what the Bible says?

_____

_____

_____

_____

Name:_____ Date:_____

CHAPTER 12: BIBLE STUDY QUESTIONS

Before Jesus came, God's people were required for follow over 600 laws. **Read the following verses** in your Bible to see a few examples of those laws.

☐ Leviticus 11:10-11   ☐ Leviticus 19:27   ☐ Leviticus 19:32

☐ Leviticus 24:16   ☐ Numbers 28:11   ☐ Numbers 29:1

When Jesus was on earth, He said He had come to fulfill the Law (Matthew 5:17). This doesn't mean that we can now follow Jesus, but do whatever we want to do with no rules. Instead, Jesus described the Law in a different way. Read what He says in Matthew 22:34-40 (NIV).

> Hearing that Jesus had silenced the Sadducees, the Pharisees got together. One of them, an expert in the law, tested him with this question: "Teacher, which is the greatest commandment in the Law?"

> Jesus replied: "'Love the Lord your God with all your heart and with all your soul and with all your mind.' This is the first and greatest commandment. And the second is like it: 'Love your neighbor as yourself.' All the Law and the Prophets hang on these two commandments."

The two commandments Jesus spoke of were part of the Law. **Read them** in your Bible: ☐ Leviticus 19:18   ☐ Deuteronomy 6:5

In other words, the Law and God's ways are about love; His love for you and your love for others. However, there was a problem with the Law. The Law could not completely take away sin (Hebrews 7:19). And it is impossible to follow the Law perfectly. Instead, the Law shows our need for Jesus and His love (Romans 3:19-20; Galatians 3:24).

Jesus fulfilled the Law, and He does what the Law could not do. He completely removes sin from our spirit and makes it possible to be with Him forever. And He says the commandments in the Bible are about love.

Jesus says to love your neighbor. **Read Luke 10:25-37**. Who is your neighbor?

_____

_____

_____

_____

Think about all the times that you should obey someone. Maybe it is obeying your parents, grandparents, teachers at school, or leaders at church. When you obey, are you obeying because you are afraid you will get in trouble if you don't? Or are you obeying because you love your neighbor?

_____

_____

_____

Jesus said, "If you love me, keep my commands" (John 14:15 NIV). If you should obey Jesus because you love Him (and not because you think you'll get in trouble), what is the reason you should also obey people such as your parents?

_____

_____

_____

www.hideandseekministries.com

WORD SCRAMBLE

_____ _____ _____ _____
   fI   ouy   olev   em
            ◇   ❀

_____ _____ _____
   uoy   liwl   obye
                          ☺

_____ _____   John 14:15 NCV
  ym   ocmamnsd
            ☆

Jesus delights in _____ and _____ .
                        ◇   ❀

To _____ Jesus' _____ is proof
         ☺   ☆

that _____ are saved.
         ◇

Name:_____ **Date:**_____

CHAPTER 13: REVIEW QUESTIONS

1. Jesus defeated _____.

2. If Jesus had not been raised from the dead _____.

    a. we would still have sin in our spirits.

    b. no one would be able to go to Heaven.

    c. the Bible would be meaningless.

    d. All of the above.

3. After Jesus died, no one ever saw Him again.

    a. True

    b. False

4. Jesus is going to return to earth again some day.

    a. True

    b. False

5. Jesus is preparing a place for you in Heaven right now.

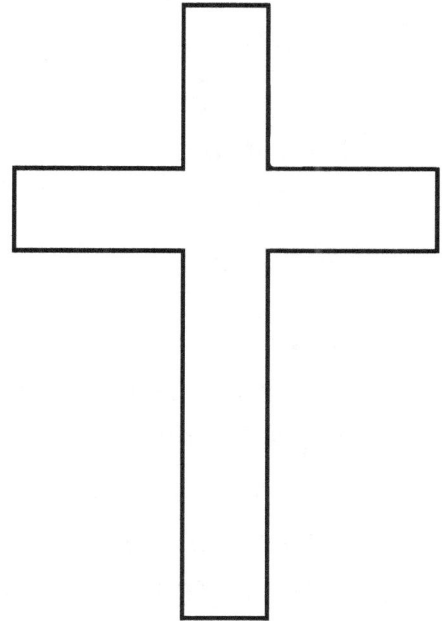

    a. True

    b. False

Name:_____ **Date:**_____

CHAPTER 13: BIBLE STUDY QUESTIONS

Imagine four people went to the beach together. They have just come back from their trip, and each one is telling you about their travels. Do you think each person would tell you exactly the same information? For example, the first person might tell you how cold the ocean was and how nice the weather was. The second person might tell you about the good seafood they ate and the crab they saw on the beach. Since the second person didn't tell you about the cold ocean, does that mean the first person was not telling you the truth? No, you are hearing about the same trip from four different perspectives; from four different people who told their story in their own way. Just because their stories do not match perfectly does not mean they are not telling the truth. They have just made different decisions on what information to tell you about.

The same is true for four books in the Bible. The books of Matthew, Mark, Luke and John are called the Gospels. They tell about Jesus' time on earth in four different perspectives. Since the books were written by four different people, something that is said about Jesus in one book may not be included in another book. Or the same story may be told with slightly different details. The amazing thing is, is that the books do not contradict each other. They work together to tell about Jesus and give us more information from different perspectives, so we can have a better understanding. Let's look at a few examples that have to do with the resurrection of Jesus.

Read Mark 16:12-13. After Jesus was raised from the dead, it says He appeared to two men as they walked into the country. But we are not told very many details.

Now, **read Luke 24:13-35.** Luke tells us about the same story of Jesus when He walked and talked with the two men. But Luke includes much more detail. What are some details that Luke tells us that Mark does not tell us?

_____

_____

_____

_____

The other two books in the Gospels (Matthew and John) do not tell about Jesus talking with the men at all. Since Mark did not include all the details that Luke did, and the other books do not include the story at all, does this mean someone was not telling the truth or the Bible is wrong? Why?

_____

_____

_____

_____

Read Luke 24:12. In this one verse, Luke tells how Peter went to the empty tomb.

Now, **read John 20:1-10**. Notice how many more details John gives than Luke does. For instance, John tells us that he went with Peter to the tomb, but Luke does not give those details. Do you think what Luke wrote and what John wrote show the Bible is not true? Or do you think Peter going to the tomb was told by two different perspectives, and we can learn more by reading both?

_____

_____

_____

CROSSWORD PUZZLE

Across

1. Jesus defeated _____.

4. When Jesus came back to life,
   He had a real _____.

5. Jesus was raised from the _____.

6. Those who believe without seeing
   are truly _____.

8. Jesus let others _____ Him.

Down

2. The angel said, "Do not be _____."

3. Jesus was buried in a rich man's _____.

7. Jesus is going to come back to _____.

Name:_____ **Date:**_____

CHAPTER 14: REVIEW QUESTIONS

1. What are some examples of clues from long ago that can tell us about what happened in history?

_____

_____

_____

_____

2. There are no clues in history that tell us about Jesus' life on earth.

    a. True

    b. False

3. How do you know Jesus really existed as a person on earth?

_____

_____

_____

_____

_____

_____

Name:_____ **Date:**_____

CHAPTER 14: BIBLE STUDY QUESTIONS

In what ways, if any, do you think the Bible is similar to a history book?

_____

_____

_____

_____

_____

_____

In what way(s) do you think the Bible is *not* like a history book?

_____

_____

_____

_____

_____

_____

_____

_____

HISTORY CODE

Use the chart to solve the message below.

	☺	♦	♪	☃	✉	✂	✝	⚑
▲	A	B	C	D	E	F	G	H
♥	I	J	K	L	M	N	O	P
☎	Q	R	S	T	U	V	X	Y

▲⚑　♥☺　☎♪　☎☃　♥✝　☎♦　☎⚑

☎☃　▲✉　♥☃　♥☃　☎♪　　☎✉　☎♪

☎☃　▲⚑　▲☺　☎☃

♥♦　▲✉　☎♪　☎✉　☎♪　　▲☃　♥☺　▲☃

▲✉　☎✝　♥☺　☎♪　☎☃

Name:_____ Date:_____

CHAPTER 15: REVIEW QUESTIONS

1. What is an archaeologist?

_____

_____

_____

2. Why is it helpful for archaeologists to find items with writing on them?

_____

_____

_____

_____

3. List three items that have been found through archaeology that have to do with the life of Jesus.

_____

_____

_____

_____

_____

_____

Name:_____ **Date:**_____

CHAPTER 15: BIBLE STUDY QUESTIONS

In Chapter 11, you read about faith. Faith is being absolutely sure about something even though you cannot see it with your eyes. And in this chapter (Chapter 15), you have read about "seeing history" with your own eyes through archaeology. If someone searches for clues about Jesus' time on earth that they can <u>see</u>, does that mean they don't have faith?

_____

It's okay if you are not sure of the answer. Here are some things to think about. Did God stay in Heaven and say, "*You must believe Me, but you can <u>never see</u> anything about Me. And I will never show anyone proof of who I am?*"

Read what the Bible says in the book of John:

> "No one has ever seen God. But the One and Only is God and is at the Father's side. The one at the Father's side has shown us what God is like." (John 1:18 NIrV).

It is true that no one has seen God. But God has not remained hidden in Heaven. Remember, God is three persons in one, and He <u>did</u> come down from Heaven through Jesus. And not only did He come down from Heaven, but He performed many signs for others to <u>see</u> with their own eyes. And the reason why the signs are written about in the Bible is so we will believe.

Read what it says in John 20:30-31 (NIV):

> "Jesus performed many other signs in the presence of his disciples, which are not recorded in this book. But these are written that you may believe that Jesus is the Messiah, the Son of God, and that by believing you may have life in his name."

Jesus performed many signs that others could see, and we get to read about them. A definition of the Greek word for "signs" in the verse above is: "an explanation of something hidden and secret".[1] So, another way we could describe it is to say a sign is a clue. The signs of Jesus are something that help explain who Jesus is, and why He came to earth. The signs were something people could <u>see</u> with their own eyes. They were clues.

Read what Jesus said in John 5:36-37 (NCV).

> "The things I do, which are the things my Father gave me to do, prove that the Father sent me. And the Father himself who sent me has given proof about me..."

God does not remain hidden, and He does not tell you that you can never see anything about Him with your own eyes. In the first book of *Hidden Treasure Quest*, we learned that we can also <u>see</u> a glimpse of God through what He has created. We are saved by having *faith* in Jesus. However, God also gives us ways to <u>see</u> who He really is with our own eyes. And archaeology is one way we can *see* the history of Jesus' time on earth. It can even help build up your faith.

Now, **read about some signs** that Jesus did in the book of John:

☐ John 2:1-11 ☐ John 4:46-54 ☐ John 5:1-14

☐ John 6:1-15 ☐ John 9:1-41 ☐ John 11:1-57

---

1 - James Strong. "The New Strong's Expanded Exhaustive Concordance of the Bible." In Greek Dictionary of the New Testament (Nashville: Thomas Nelson Publishers, 2001), 226.

SECRET Code

Use the *Knowing God Through Jesus* book to solve the code below.

Below are groups of three numbers. Each group of numbers represents one word in the book. Here is what the numbers in each group mean:

First number = The page number in the book.

Second number = The line on the page. (Count all the lines with words on them including the titles in bold.)

Third number = The Word in the line.

Once you find a word in the book, write it on the line above the numbers.

_____   _____   _____
    93, 1, 4   9, 6, 1   19, 6, 2

_____   _____   _____
   33, 2, 10   87, 19, 6   93, 5, 2

_____   _____   _____
   79, 18, 7   112, 2, 2   67, 10, 5

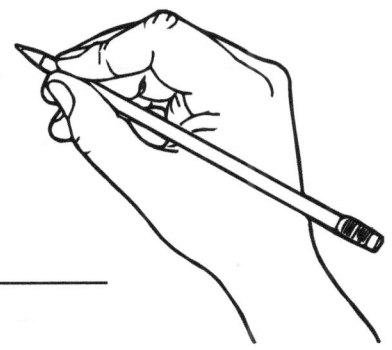

Name: _____ **Date:** _____

CHAPTER 16: REVIEW QUESTIONS

1. Is the Bible just another clue in history? _____

2. Sometimes God does things that do not make sense with our human understanding.

    a. True

    b. False

3. If you choose not to believe unless you can see a clue, then it's like you are Peter looking at the wind and the waves.

    a. True

    b. False

4. Jesus asked, "But who do you say that I am?" (Mark 8:29 NKJV). Who do *you* say Jesus is?

_____

_____

_____

_____

_____

Name:_____ **Date:**_____

CHAPTER 16: BIBLE STUDY QUESTIONS

Read 2 Kings 5:1-19. Namaan was a man with a skin disease. A servant girl told Naaman he should see a prophet named Elisha, and Naaman agreed to see him.

What did Elisha's messenger tell Naaman to do?

_____

_____

_____

How did Naaman react when Elisha's messenger told him to do that?

_____

_____

_____

When Naaman went to see Elisha, Naaman had his own thoughts about what he expected Elisha to do. Naaman said: "I thought Elisha would surely come out and stand before me and call on the name of the Lord his God. I thought he would wave his hand over the place and heal the disease" (2 Kings 5:11 NCV). But what Naaman thought Elisha would do was much different than what Elisha actually did.

Elisha did not even meet Naaman. Instead, Elisha told a messenger to tell Naaman to wash in the Jordan River seven times. This did not make sense to Naaman. And not only did Naaman not understand, but it made him angry.

What happened after Naaman obeyed and he dipped in the Jordan seven times?

_____

What do you think would have happened if Naaman would have dipped in a different river or only dipped three times instead of seven?

_____

_____

Even though dipping in the Jordan did not make sense to Naaman, it worked. Naaman was healed. Sometimes God does things that do not make sense with our human understanding, and we have to trust and obey Him anyway.

Can you think of other stories in the Bible where God told someone to do something, but they did not understand or it did not make sense to them?

_____

_____

_____

_____

_____

_____

KEEP YOUR FOCUS

Lead Peter through the maze and help him focus on
Jesus by avoiding the wind and the waves.

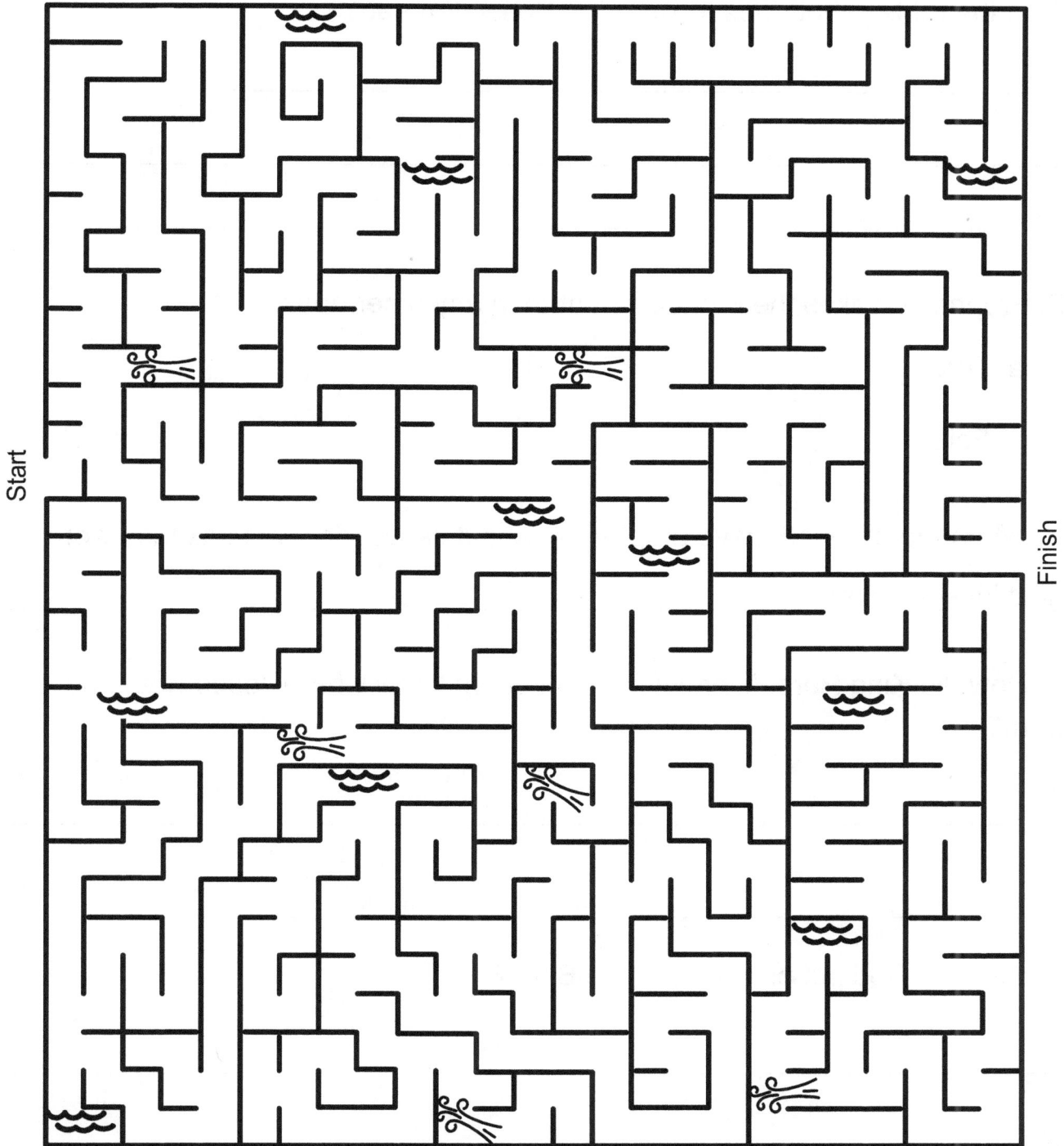

Name: _____ **Date:** _____

CHAPTER 17: REVIEW QUESTIONS

1. In the Bible, what does the word "prophecy" mean?

_____

_____

_____

2. Prophecy makes the Bible different than any other book.

    a. True

    b. False

3. When the prophets gave prophecies about Jesus, do you think they were

just lucky guesses?_____

4. How did King Herod's priests and teachers know where Jesus would be born?

_____

_____

5. Why did God put prophecy in the Bible?

_____

_____

_____

Name:_____ **Date:**_____

CHAPTER 17: BIBLE STUDY QUESTIONS

Prophecy is a message from God about the future. In the Bible, let's read a few of the prophecies about Jesus in the Old Testament (written hundreds of years before Jesus was born). Then, let's read when it was fulfilled (came true) in the New Testament (hundreds of years later).

First **read**: ☐ Psalm 41:9. Then **read**: ☐ Luke 22:47-48.

First **read**: ☐ Zechariah 11:12. Then **read**: ☐ Matthew 26:14-15.

First **read**: ☐ Isaiah 50:6. Then **read**: ☐ Matthew 26:67.

Now, **read** this prophecy that is given in the Old Testament: ☐ Zechariah 9:9.

Look in the New Testament of your Bible and try to find where this prophecy was fulfilled. Write the Bible verse reference on the line below. (Hint: It can be found in any of the four Gospels.)

_____

Read Appendix D in the *Knowing God Through Jesus* book (page 123).

Many of the prophecies about the end of the world are found in the book of Revelation (the last book in the Bible). In Revelation, it says God will one day make a new Heaven and a new earth. There will also be a holy city in Heaven that we will get to enjoy. Read the following verses in your Bible to find out more.

☐ Revelation 21:1-27

☐ Revelation 22:1-5

Will there be a sea in Heaven? _____

Wil there be a sun or a moon in Heaven? _____

Will there be night in Heaven? _____

Will anyone ever cry in Heaven? _____

Who will be standing at the 12 gates of the New Jerusalem? _____

_____

What will the gates be made of? _____

What will the streets in the city be made of? _____

_____

What are some things you are looking forward to when you get to Heaven?

_____

_____

_____

_____

_____

_____

_____

HEAVEN

Draw a picture of some things you are looking forward to in Heaven.

Name:_____ **Date:**_____

CHAPTER 18

FINAL REVIEW QUESTIONS

The following questions are a review of all 18 chapters.

1. In Matthew 7:13-14, it says there are two roads that people choose to follow. What are the two roads?

   1. _____

   2. _____

2. God is speaking to you right now.

   a. True

   b. False

3. When Jesus looks at people, He looks at _____.

   a. the way they look

   b. how many things they have

   c. their heart

4. The Bible says, "This is how we know what _____ is: Jesus Christ laid down his life for us" (1 John 3:16 NIV).

   a. God's Word

   b. love

   c. the Holy Spirit

5. Jesus said all people who believe in Him are the _____ of the world.

    a. light

    b. darkness

6. List some things you can do to seek God. (Read pages 28-29 in Chapter 5.)

_____

_____

_____

_____

_____

7. List some things in life that can distract you.

_____

_____

_____

_____

8. List seven reasons why we should pray. (You can find them in Chapter 7.)

    1. _____

    2. _____

    3. _____

    4. _____

5. _____

6. _____

7. _____

9. Where does God hide His wisdom and knowledge?

a. He buried them in the ground.

b. He hid them in Jesus.

c. It's a secret. No one knows.

10. While Jesus was on earth, He said He can only do what He sees God do. (In other words, if you want to know what God is like, read about the life of Jesus.)

a. True

b. False

11. There is one body of Christ (His Church), but there are many different _____.

a. parts

b. feet

c. spirits

12. The faith that comes from God works with your five senses.

a. True

b. False

13. Why should you do what the Bible says?

_____

_____

_____

_____

14. If Jesus had not been raised from the dead _____.

    a. we would still have sin in our spirits.

    b. no one would be able to go to Heaven.

    c. the Bible would be meaningless.

    d. All of the above.

15. There are no clues in history that tell us about Jesus' life on earth.

    a. True

    b. False

16. How do you know Jesus really existed as a person on earth?

_____

_____

_____

_____

_____

17. Why did God put prophecy in the Bible?

_____

_____

_____

_____

18. Jesus asked, "But who do you say that I am?" (Mark 8:29 NKJV). Who do _you_ say Jesus is?

_____

_____

_____

_____

Name:_____ Date:_____

CHAPTER 18: BIBLE STUDY QUESTIONS

This study guide has been helping you learn about God through Jesus. Jesus is the Son of God, but He is also God. When you learn about Jesus, you are also learning about God. And as you search through the Bible as if searching for a hidden treasure, you will find out "how to know God" (Proverbs 2:1-5 NIrV). You will also learn how to be a disciple of Jesus: a person who listens to, learns from, and follows Jesus Christ.

In this book, we have been reading about finding and following the will of God. In other words, how to find, follow, and stay on God's path for your life. This will not always be easy to do. We have so many choices to make every day, and many of those choices will decide whether you stay on God's path.

Jesus said, "I am the way and the truth and the life" (John 14:6 NIV). Jesus is the one and only way. To every choice you make say, *what would Jesus do?* Or, *what would Jesus want me to do?* His way is always what is best for you. And as you make an effort to follow His way, remember who you are. You are a child of God!

Read Ephesians 2 in your Bible. Then write some notes below about what Jesus as done for you, and what it means to be a child of God.

_____

_____

_____

_____

_____

_____

_____

_____

_____

_____

_____

_____

_____

_____

_____

_____

_____

For more Bible activities:

Go to www.hideandseekministries.com/printables to find activity pages that are free to download and print.

OTHER BOOKS IN
THE HIDDEN TREASURE QUEST SERIES

1. *Knowing God Through Creation*
2. *Knowing God Through Jesus*
3. *Knowing God Through the Holy Spirit*

HSM PODCAST

The Knowing God Podcast for Kids
Available on most podcasting apps and the HSM website.

BENJAMIN NEARY

Do you enjoy Ben's stories in the *Hidden Treasure Quest* series? Read more about Ben's life in this exciting, page-turning mystery with lovable characters and underlying Christian themes. Available in paperback and eBook. Perfect for ages nine and up.

www.hideandseekministries.com

www.ingramcontent.com/pod-product-compliance
Lightning Source LLC
Chambersburg PA
CBHW081240020426
42331CB00013B/3236